LAND OF TALES

POEMS

Kraftgriots

Also in the series (POETRY)

David Cook *et al*: *Rising Voices*
Olu Oguibe: *A Gathering Fear;* winner, 1992 All Africa Okigbo Prize for Literature
      & Honourable mention, 1993 Noma Award for Publishing in Africa
Nnimmo Bassey: *Patriots and Cockroaches*
Okinba Launko: *Dream-Seeker on Divining Chain*
Onookome Okome: *Pendants,* winner, 1993 ANA/Cadbury poetry prize
Nnimmo Bassey: *Poems on the Run*
Ebereonwu: *Suddenly God was Naked*
Tunde Olusunle: *Fingermarks*
Joe Ushie: *Lambs at the Shrine*
Chinyere Okafor: *From Earth's Bedchamber*
Ezenwa-Ohaeto: *The Voice of the Night Masquerade,* joint-winner, 1997 ANA,
      Cadbury poetry prize
George Ehusani: *Fragments of Truth*
Remi Raji: *A Harvest of Laughters,* joint-winner 1997 ANA/Cadbury poetry prize
Patrick Ebewo: *Self-Portrait & Other Poems*
George Ehusani: *Petals of Truth*
Nnimmo Bassey: *Intercepted*
Joe Ushie: *Eclipse in Rwanda*
Femi Oyebode: *Selected Poems*
Ogaga Ifowodo: *Homeland & Other Poems,* winner, 1993 ANA poetry prize
Godwin Uyi Ojo: *Forlorn Dreams*
Tanure Ojaide: *Delta Blues and Home Songs*
Niyi Osundare: *The Word is an Egg* (2000)
Tayo Olafioye: *A Carnival of Looters* (2000)
Ibiwari Ikiriko: *Oily Tears of the Delta* (2000)
Arnold Udoka: *I Am the Woman* (2000)
Akinloye Ojo: *In Flight* (2000)
Joe Ushie: *Hill Songs* (2000)
Ebereonwu: *The Insomniac Dragon* (2000)
Deola Fadipe: *I Make Pondripples* (2000)
Remi Raji: *Webs of Remembrance* (2001)
'Tope Omoniyi: *Farting Presidents and Other Poems* (2001)
Tunde Olusunle: *Rhythm of the Mortar* (2001)
Abdullahi Ismaila: *Ellipsis* (2001)
Tayo Olafioye: *The Parliament of Idiots: Tryst of the* Sinators (2002)
Femi Abodunrin: *It Would Take Time: Conversation with Living Ancestors* (2002)
Nnimmo Bassey: *We Thought It Was Oil But It Was Blood* (2002)
Ebi Yeibo: *A Song For Tomorrow and Other Poems* (2003)
Adebayo Lamikanra: *Heart Sounds* (2003)
Ezenwa-Ohaeto: *The Chants of a Minstrel* (2003), winner, 2004 ANA/NDDC poetry
      prize and joint-winner, 2005 LNG The Nigeria Prize for Literature
Seyi Adigun: *Kalakini: Songs of Many Colours* (2004)
Ebi Yeibo: *Maiden Lines* (2004)
Funso Aiyejina: *I, The Supreme & Other Poems* (2004)
'Lere Oladitan: *Boolekaja: Lagos Poems 1* (2005)
Seyi Adigun: *Bard on the Shore* (2005)
Famous Dakolo: *A Letter to Flora* (2005)
Olawale Durojaiye: *An African Night* (2005)

LAND OF TALES

POEMS

Barth Akpah

kraftgriots

Published by

Kraft Books Limited
6A, Polytechnic Road, Sango, Ibadan
Box 22084, University of Ibadan Post Office
Ibadan, Oyo State, Nigeria
℡ +234 (0)803 348 2474, +234 (0)805 129 1191
+234 (0)803 350 9421, +234 (0)905 723 9357
E-mail: kraftbooks@yahoo.com;
kraftbookslimited@gmail.com
Website: www.kraftbookslimited.com

First published 2019

ISBN 978–978–918–553–5

= KRAFTGRIOTS =
(A literary imprint of Kraft Books Limited)

First printing, April 2019

On this marble of dedication

I celebrate

Chukwu Okike, the source of all breaths, whose words have always come to be, in seasons and out of it, and for the seasoning added unto my tales.

He weaved me into a being that my tales would come to be

And

My late father, late Chief Akpah Onyeaboh. Many mouths spoke of your words, worlds and tales.

On this marble of thanksgiving and praise

I remember, first, many that washed my feet, many that minted my words and cast them into medals. My voice came from the Supreme Being, Lord the giver of life. I appreciate my sweet muse stable, my mum, who held me in her hands like a bird and set me free into the air to sail. Yet, she kept vigil and made her prayers a paladin for my safety. I acknowledge my Big Brother, Chief Michael Akpah and his wife, Chief Mrs Helen Akpah, for the nature and nurture.

I thank Dr Elliot Wreh Wilson, Emeritus Professor, Edinboro University, Pennsylvania, U.S.A and current President of William V. S. Tubman University for his love of art and artistry. My gratitude also goes to all the good shepherds of my creative writing – Profs Remi Raji, Ademola Dasylva, Remi Oriaku, Ayo Kehinde, Babatunde Omobowale, Nelson Fashina, Hyginus Ekwuazi, Adenike Akinjobi and Oluwatoyin Jegede of the University of Ibadan literary circle. I also say thank you to Professor Patricia Jabbeh Wesley of the Department of English, Pen State University, U.S. who despite her busy schedule did a critical assessment of the manuscript. I equally treasure Professor Obododimma Oha of the Department of English, University of Ibadan, Nigeria, who accepted to write the foreword to this collection under very short notice. These noble men and women have led me into the fresh water of muse; I drank and I'm still drinking!

This collection in its early stage has passed through the eye of many other needles. I appreciate the efforts of the following whose suggestions further added a taste to this work. To this, I appreciate Mr Tade Ipadeola and Mr Olatoyese Jayeoba, Drs Ibukun Filani, Stephen kekeghe, James Yeku and Abayomi Awelewa. I also appreciate Mr Henry Akubuiro, Ndubuisi Martins, Mrs Kaliatu George and Oladimeji Ramon. Similarly, I appreciate Professor Mlee Too Wesley, Dean, College of Arts and Sciences, Professor Isaac Adetunde, College of Engineering and Technology and also Professor Amanze Ihedioha, Dean, College of Education all from Tubman University, Liberia. My lyrics of praise swim also to Rev. Sunday Dawodu, the Chair, Department of Language and Literature, and Professor William Harris, the Director, Center for Excellence in

Teaching and Learning, W.V.S.T.U., Liberia and my colleagues in the Department of Language and Literature, College of Arts and Sciences, William V.S Tubman University, Harper, Liberia: Professors Oscar Dickerson, John Dio Kimber III, Henry Woart and Jerry Nwagbe for their encouragements. Charles Akintunde of College of Engineering, T.U., thanks for all the smiles and support.

I have always perched on trees which serve as 'museful' refuge. To these trees, especially my uncle, Mr Chris Ogbonna, Ifunanya, and my siblings, you're all phenomenal.

Poet's exordium

My thoughts run to an end
without end …
It ferries my being
without me.

My root breathes in the waters
of the *gods at the harvest*
and *harvest of laughters*
but I seek not the many laughters
in *waiting laughters*.

My songs ferment in *songs of odamolugbe*
long birthed in Abule Ilagbe:
now in *seasons of rage*
seeking not *a mirage* …

Poetry gave me voice in stillness. My tears drop in its rhythms and upon its wings I weave melodies of wor(l)ds. It is a song and laughter of many shades. Poetry is artistic boorishness against rodents; it is a gild for word peckers at love handles.

Without gilding the lily, Oduma and the little village, Abule Ilagbe of the East-West wings, sewed calmness and gave me beauty for word carving; IBADAN clattering inspired matters and manners of the word in its blank spaces to a new world of flipping poops. Room 32 and the Faculty quadrangle where many legs and voices gave birth to words by the word masters were newsrooms for poetry and her offspring. From my paternal weaning to the waters that bathe my feet across life's journeys, I enjoy the pleasures of words in its varieties and the poetry they birth. In these verses are tales of nations. The poems in these matters are breathing tales and

tongues mustering truths in pains
steered by pogroms and rabbinics;
instincts of deaths which grace my eyes
and swam my thoughts
in noisy silence of thunderous voice.

And now my fingers called to plant
caricaturing phrases of plain mysteries.
and the love riddles that close the tales.

Foreword

Writing a foreword to a book is a gesture that suggests that one subscribes to the content and the style in some clear ways. In a sense, it is a kind of testimonial strategy; it means that one identifies with what the author is saying. It is not a mere marketing strategy meant to enhance the testimonial of the work. I have read the poems in *Land of Tales* and do like them. It is important for me to say why I endorse the collection. Perhaps the honour of being asked to write this foreword would also add to my own testimonial!

It is obvious that I am highly impressed by the poems in *Land of Tales* to want to pen this foreword. One could start right from the title to see how this poet makes us curious, makes one to know more. I know that poets like indirect language or try to mask their language, in order to accomplish that important task of demonstrating a craft in language. So, "land" and "tales" may not be what we know them to be. Even if they are, which "land" and what types of "tales"? The "land" I would thank my stars for being born into or curse? The types of "tales" I would like to listen to or hate to be subjected to? Whose "tales," by the way? Who is the teller, the implied author? Are they the kind of tales an aged uncle would finish telling the audience close to midnight and one would like to sleep close to one's mother? All the same, "land of tales" raises my curiosity as a title.

In addition, one is coming from a background where tales matter. Almost everything has a tale linked to it or is a tale of its own. With tales, we are taught and do understand better. With tales, we know where we are coming from and where we could be headed. Our personal names are tales. Our community names are tales. Our daily lives are tales linked to other tales. Individually and communally, we are tales. Wasn't that why Africa's ancestors created festivals?

Tales remind us about the structures of life, for they begin somewhere, have twists and turns inside, and end somewhere. We are mindful of roles we play in these twists and turns of collective tales. That is also why poets like Barth Akpah should not stifle their voices for they have an important role to play in this structuring of the collective tale!

Another point one must make is the influence of other voices in our articulation of this collective tale. I believe this is one reason Akpah in his introduction pays homage to Ibadan and some griots at the university:

Without gilding the lily, Oduma and the little village, Abule Ilagbe of the East-West wings sewed calmness and gave me beauty for word carving; IBADAN clattering inspired matters and manners of the word in its blank spaces to a new world of flipping poops. Room 32 and the Faculty quadrangle where many legs and voices gave birth to words by the word masters were newsrooms for poetry and her offspring. From my paternal weaning to the waters that bathe my feet across life journeys, I enjoy the pleasures of words in its varieties and the poetry they birth. In these verses are nations of tales.

One thing that attracts one's attention is the representation of language in the poem, the very material in use, as not just sculpted to create situations or contexts, but also as an aviator:

… words flown into winds,
Careering with ease
To mould words into worlds
And weave matter into matters
And unfurl the burden of matters.
    ("Matters")

This interest in language is not surprising; the poet does it with language, with signification. If it is not to make the message unique, it is for aesthetic reasons. Even the aesthetic, the craft accomplished through language, might be just another way of confirming that this is really an ARTIST and that he pays attention to his medium.

Of course, it is a learning process, in crafting words. Lucky are those who find masters that can mentor them. The poet articulates this learning experience well, writing in "Like a bird" as follows:

This chickadee is fledgling for a flight
With metaphors of the tongue.
Spreads its wings with words
Breathing in volumes of tales ….

Is it not worthwhile to examine how the poet derives and uses resources in this experience with language in the learning process? Certainly. I looked for that and took interest in "On the street of dream," one of the poems in the section, "Anthems of Fame." This conversational poem is the type we often find in many African folklore, one entity — maybe even an abstract entity — conversing with another thing, and at the end we learn lessons from the exchange. In other words, the entities could be representative of positions, may be allegorical. In the conversation, however, the experience is made contemporary: Eagle (often associated with nobility) converses with Bat, which in Igbo folklore is associated with hybridity: it is neither a bird of the air nor a four-footed animal that walks the ground. It is neither here nor there! Eagle invites Bat to various kinds of sports — actually tries to be as persuasive as possible — but Bat also advances reasons — indeed excuses — for not wanting to participate. Of course, Bat is equally persuasive, but we can see right away that his excuses are lame; they spring out of poor logic. If a neighbour's nephew loses a knee cap in the arena while playing soccer or the sharks normally do breakfast with the flesh of human swimmers and Ajakaye lost some molars while boxing, it does not follow that Bat would have the same sad experiences. Bat could be a champion. You see: that is why Bat is a bat; neither here nor there! But this effectively underlines the importance of logic in our various forms of rhetoric.

What is even particularly interesting is the attempt at crafting this fictive conversation from a folkloric bent, linking rhetoric and logic in conversation, modern sports (the enchantment of many!) with the traditional setting, and the metaphorical with personification as tropes.

There is, of course, that tendency by a poet as a master of words, to try to mesmerize us by presenting the abstract as if it were concrete, the distant as what is near, in the aesthetic engagement. In "To what end," we have the following:

To what end are the laughters
That stipple the colours of our tears?
To what end are the dances
That bid us farewell to the battle lines
To what end the smiles

That played deaf to the rhythms of our joys?
To what end the words
That failed the mind's tangles?

You see the magic in linking laughter with painting (colours) and colours with joy! No modern technology will try to reflect those moods in emoticons. They remain poetic flights of fancy, exacted in slippery language!

In the section, "Anthem of the State," we are confronted with responses to experiences on contemporary global politics. I am particularly attracted to the poem, "I need a word" which says:

I need a word to swim across the Atlantic Ocean
Erect manses on the Red Sea
Snuggle the sun with a royal kiss
And speak in the moon's tongue.
I need a word

I need a word
To touch the nipples of Monica
Without Clinton's rod across the sea
Dance *Atilogwu*
In the altar of saints.
I need a word

The poet takes a panoramic view of unfortunate happenings in global politics, with America, of course, at the centre of it all!

I was looking out for the despair that is seen in the discourses of many from the disadvantaged part of the world. I found it in "Andante." The poet laments there:

The stars have refused to twinkle
In protest of a wailing land.
The moon blinks its eyes,
Against the earth whose heart is broken.

....

Do we need more? Indeed, some countries are obviously heart-broken over the litany of problems that come their way, especially the kind of leadership and retrogression they run into. Is it not surprising that their leadership is far away from their dreams? He writes further:

Our king's palace is a hill upon which tales erupt,
Giving birth to herding songs,
Moving and adopting motions of anomy,
And implantations of Shylock pains,
And deaths that refuse to be beaten....

How so well some African countries in travail fit into this sad picture? It is appropriate that the poem is classified under "Anthems of the State." Is it not paradoxical that a dirge is an anthem, just as an anthem is a dirge in such a land of despair? Is your national anthem just a dirge? Who is dead? The country? Isn't that one of the important tales in that Land of Tales, your tales?

Honestly, memory is important. Do we remember to remember or remember to forget? The poem "The Mongers" in the collection helps me to remember that. One of the interesting verses says:

Remember...
The hunger
That torments our bellies
The thirst
That dries our tongues
The darkness
That chases our light
The bullets
That chase our breaths
The quakes
That bury our bones
....

It is an endless litany of woes. There is a lot to remember to remember! In all, the centre is that darkness is driving away the light, helping us to remember the original "Let there be light" speech act that the creator performed. That was in the days when you could still change reality with language, with words!

Let me quickly point out that this volume of poems has the outlook expected: it twists with pain and drips with blood. That is one good reason to spend a good moment on the stanza that says:
Bring back our days

When birds make nests unguided
Our light clips the lips of darkness, truth overcoming shadows
Our men stand firm on words and honours; women keep their homes

And children, the innocent hopes of our lands,
and the land dances with us.

Something, other than nostalgia, is waiting to be addressed. I expect the men standing firm on words to match that with appropriate action and not substitute the words with the deceit of the season.

Prof. Obododimma Oha
Professor of Cultural Semiotics & Stylistics,
Department of English,
University of Ibadan.

Contents

On this marble of dedication 5
On this marble of thanksgiving and praise 6
Poet's exordium 8
Foreword 10

ANTHEMS OF DREAMS 19
Thirst 20
Like a bird 22
Matters 23
Caprice ... Ruptured 24
Truth 25

ANTHEMS OF FAME 27
Man and fame 28
Reflections I 29
Reflections II 30
The land of locusts .... pang 31
On the street of dream 32
Bachelors' tale 34
To what end? ... Vain? 37

ANTHEMS OF STATE 39
Dolour 40
I want to sing 42
Andante 43
Allegro ... Opus 44
Fix, muddle 45
Words and opposites 46
Songs of GADAFI 48
I need a word 50
The bawling for Biafra 51
Death kiss 52
Words that muffled the land 53
Weep not ... Dashed 54
The mongers 55

Unwanted songs 56
Your cast 58
Parrymentarians 59
Soka! 60
Book a ram, kill a ram 61
The dance 62
Letter to mr president 64
Re: letter to mr president 67
Letter to mama ... the pains that ache our land 70
Trump-Kim ... A dance before us 72
Battle lines ... Red lines 73
Brothers at war ... Fissures 74
A new song 75
Today for tomorrow 76
Niger area ... a country was 77
Come, laughter come ... Gone 78
Osun dance of victory 79
To the last end 80
Nature's smile 81
Independence ... Lost song 82
How to live ... illusion 83
The pride of laughter 84
Lost 85
2019 ... 2015? ... 2023? ... 2019 86
Petepete ... the pain of our hearts 87
Hard lines ... Red lines 88

ANTHEMS OF THE HEART 89
Heart beats 90
Silent night 91
Ify 92
Emeka's chase 93
Mascara 94
Sayonara 95

ANTHEMS OF DREAMS

Thirst

This
is
me
mouth gaping
for
a drop
of water ...

This
is
me
mouth gaping
for
a goblet
of verse ...

This
is
me
thought
crossed
and
I,
emissary
of
the
muse
and
the
mute
invading
flood
of
thoughts

in
the
land
of
tales

Like a bird ...

The chickadee is fledgling for a flight
with metaphors of words.
Spreads its wings with words
breathing in volumes of tales,
luffing across the tides;
its feet webbed to paddle what
its eyes saw as rivers ...

Like a raven, the word flies and perches,
transcending boundaries and colours.
flying on the wings of songs;
ruffling the world's feathers
freighted on the beak of melodies
and firmament of its air, its talons
of worlds and words in wells
of tales seeking voice
for many that seek its rhythms
before its flight.

Matters

...words flown into the winds,
careering with ease
to mould words into worlds
and weave matter into matters
And unfurl the burden of matters.

For the world's eyes
must see how the lion wept
in the venter of a lizard and street
urchins chase palace heirs
and the jig, the comeuppance,
the tale that ensues ...

Caprice

I want to write haiku about Saul named Paul
but the road to Damascus seeks my blindness.
I want to make a chalet for love
but in me breathe melodies of hate.
I want to sing acappella for forgiveness,
but the vengeance in me dances *kunkere*…
I want to write a poem about mercy
but my heart tore my kindness apart.

I want to stipple the equality of all men
but songs of freeborns and the slaves land off key.
I want to write epos on unity
but the two divides trade with divorce.
I want to plant samba for the UNITED NATIONS
but my songs fail the Jews and Arabs.
I want to erect a marble condo for honesty,
but the land is filled with avarice.

Ruptured

Saul named Paul…
seeks my blindness.
A chalet for love…
breathe melodies of hate.
Acappella for forgiveness…
dances *kunkere*…
… A poem about mercy…
tore my kindness apart.

Equality of all men…
land off key
Epos on unity…
trade with divorce.
Samba for the United Nations…
fail the Jews and the Arabs.
A marble condo for honesty
is filled with avarice.

Truth

You are man's satirical butt.
Your voice waddles among men on the lonely
path.
The only mortals' naked fire;
the slug that haunts every dying breath,
and witnesses to secrets behind closets.

Indeed, mortals' sun.
But why do men and women
who fly your kite get docked and loathed
and those who abhor your charm
enjoy princely latria?
Why do men of all walks favour the other cheek?
Or, was it not your virtues that are sermonised
in the auricle of many at the sanctuary?

And yet, you are like a punnet,
waiting endlessly for the water's
overflow. Yet,
the other cheek's yurt is
decorated.

Even those who scrunch atop our destinies
amble not in your light.
Only a few choose your paseo
while many seek you in half measures.
Oh! I do not wish to say: you lie catnapping
as your seeds are grown but to termites'
slop.

ANTHEMS OF FAME

Man and fame

They say,
you are gifted with Carson's knife.
They say,
your thoughts flow in Wordsworth's ink.
They say,
your oratory measures Cicero's tongue.
They say,
you pace in Bolt's track.
They say,
you run the rings like Pele.
They say,
your voice sails in Jackson's serenades.
But they didn't say,
your wand speaks the ocean's heart.
and calm the waxing of its lyrics.

Reflections I

I will go the way of tsunamis;
in the deep ocean surge,
I will swim home
the tide
in soothing tales
of pleasant sins.

I will go the way of tornadoes;
in the air raid,
I will strike home
the hopes
of hopeless saints.

I will go the way of fire;
in the flickering rage,
I will smoke dry
the faded hopes
of painless pains.

But when the Sun rises,
shall I rise
in pleasant sins?
in the guidance
of hopeless saints
and tales of painless pains?

Reflections II

Morning and Night meld
at the birth of Sorrow
chasing laughter to the grave...

The Sun and Moon meld
to sing death to nature's call
with ashes crowned
for the Call ...

The Earth is pregnant
with darkness and light;
but death hosts delivery
at labour ...

The soul of man is pierced
with many arguments
tattooed on the lips
of pallbearers ...

The land of locusts

Dissonance built a ménage
and planted spikelet in our homes.

The land is heavy with termites
and seething mass of hawks festering
on the land's soul.

A country is born
at the death of honour;
now hatred reigns, and the obloquy that

swims …

pang

a ménage
  in our homes
    with
      termites,
       hawks,
        festering
         on the
          land's
           soul,
            is born

              of honour,
            and the obloquy
           that
        s
      w
     i
    m
  s
   .
  .
 .

On the street of dream

Eagle:
Come let's play soccer;
it breathes vim into your biceps
invigorates your veins
your heart feels its tonic
and makes you sit
at the table of men
and with much moolah
to fondle …

Bat:
Me? Ah! My neighbour's nephew
broke the cap of his knees
the other day at
the arena.
Now, he hobbles
to his grandmother's village
at the scornful and
pitying eyes of neighbours.

Eagle:
Then, let's go swimming,
the doctor says:
it is the game of all body parts,
it nourishes the soul
and adds humour to your days.

Bat:
Friend, my arms are
too frail to compete
with scrod of the sea
and the ocean creatures.
They say:
the human soul is a
ready-made tiffin
for the Shark!

Look my amigo,
what shall it profit me
to lose my body and soul
in the belly of a shark?

Eagle:
Okay, let's try boxing.
They say:
It spins boodles in seconds,
makes you,
a heavy weight tale
in the neighbourhood
and draws you accolades ...

Bat:
Haba! I was told:
Ajakaye's molars got missing
the other day
at the bus conductor's fist
and Holyfield's ear danced
in the bosom of Tyson's jaw
I need my ears
to herald the trumpet at dawn.

Eagle:
Are you aware of Messi's visit to village square tomorrow?

Bat:
Ah! Messi the Great.
You mean Messi?
The one whose magic
kept a million eyes glued to the screen,
I shall keep a vigil for his arrival
and pray his autograph
seals my dream
for the years to come.

Bachelors' tale

I will marry a judge
Her circumlocutions tickle my fantasy.
In her company, my pride swells.
I will numb the enemy's nose
Not for me tales of injustice
For her tongue carols my innocence.

But
Late night files are a routine
As my jaws ache in warring consonants
And pauciloquent vowels.
Now, divorce staring at me ...

I will marry a cop
Her uniform lends power to my voice
Her transfer window
A space for bachelors' freedom
Her pen and paper read meanings
To the mind's constructs.
For my safety
Hidden dens exposed
Tales from crime desk
A therapy against tyrant insomnia.

But
A couple's beef:
Curries handcuff at my door.
Sudden warrant is inevitable.
What about the prying eyes
Of *ogas* at the top?
Bulging pajamas ...
My soul grows tizzy.

I will marry a teacher
Her Mother Teresa's heart
Still my stubborn farts
And calms the nerves

My kids' tomorrow secured
Thanks to her chastening
Her smiles glow in a token
Of 'Becoming a Hero in the Teaching
Profession'.

But
Lesson notes take the night
As I nuzzle the pillow
Her unsolicited similes
Poke at my IQ
Giving me the jitters.

I will marry an actress
And enjoy the clicks of paparazzi
And centre spreads of the tabloids
Her lamprophony so soothing to a million ears.
Nightfall brings me joy as head of glamour girl

But
Jealousy tugs at my heart
With her unending presence on locations
As gossip mills tear my secrets to shreds
At the tables of a million ears
And scornful eyes.

I will marry a banker
Her green hat fits my lofty dreams
Instant loans without collateral certified.

But
The in-laws call me a gold digger
As my heart falters
Sometimes I may disconnect
In the labyrinths of her balance sheet.

I will marry a nurse
Her holy linen speaks to the eyes
My ailing veins arise
Succour in her needles
She unlocks the mojo

In 'the other room'
But
I detest lonely nightshifts
Gory tales from the wards
Alarm my resolve

Then, I will marry a slob
And sip my night away in the bar

To what end?   Vain?

To what end are the laughters   The laughters
That stipple the colours of our tears?   of our tears
To what end is the dance   dance
That bids us farewell to the battle lines?   to the battle lines.

                                                 .

To what end are the smiles   The smiles
That play deaf to the rhythms of our joys?   of our joys
To what end are words   are words
That fail the mind's tangles?   that fail the mind's tangles

To what end are the land's gods and goddesses   gods and goddesses
That lost appetite and feign nescience   feign nescience
To the land's offerings   to the land's offerings
And the fardel of her tales?   and the fardel of her tales.

ANTHEMS OF STATE

Dolour

we are the modern victims
of
Pains.
.
.

our bones dance to
Death
Rays.
.
.

our eyes saw blood in colours
of
deaths.
.
.

ferrying sands into the ocean
of
... grief

there is rumble in the spirit
of
the
... land

A kingdom that dwells
on
a
... river

wails
in
search
of water
in
.

                    the   .
                        air.

signifying
            dead-
                woods,
                    ciphers
as lion kings.
                    .

                .

I want to sing ...

I want to sing a song
Of the son and the sun
A song of the son,
Diminuting his rising with the sun.

I want to sing a song
Of the myth and the muse
Revolting songs of their mute.

I want to sing a song
Of the canary and the ravens
Sprawling to destinations unknown.

I want to sing a song
Of the mornings, the mournings and the more news
Mourning the mornings with more news.

I want to sing a song
Of the tortoise and the serpent
Both nailed in wiles.

Andante

The stars have refused to twinkle
In protest of a wailing land.
The moon blinks its eyes
Against the earth whose heart is broken.

The sun is deprived of its rays;
The earth erupts in a wailing adagio;
Its heart, an enclave of tales,
Tales of a land without eyes,
Tales of muted tongues,
Tales of brownish grass beneath our feet.

Our king's palace is a hill upon which tales erupt,
Giving birth to herding songs,
Moving and adopting motions of anomy,
And nidations of shylock pains,
And deaths that refused to be beaten …

Allegro

I plead for the glory of the sun.
I seek the beauty of the moon.
Let the earth sing for me *Oh Happy Day*
That my soul shall behold the sun, the moon
And the Earth's philia.

I crave the honour of the morning
I seek the swank of the day
My soul searches the night's caressing hands
That my breath be bathed with the afflatus of

Morning, Day and Night.

Opus

The sun, the moon
Sing for me
Oh
Happy
Day.

The morning, the day
searches the night's
caressing
hands.

Fix   Muddle

The sea is divided between the shepherd and the sheep;
Between a hireling and the sheep.
The shepherd splits his blood for the sheep
While the wolf seeks his thirst from the sheep.
But the hireling flees to his hideout,
When the tide beckons against the sheep.
The sheep are at a fix …
Standing before the two faces and togs
Of the land's god – a shepherd and a hireling.
Now the sheep bleat in search of a shepherd.
But, the Trojan horse lies in wait.

The sheep, the sheep
the sheep from the sheep
flees to his hideout against
the sheep at a fix.

Two faces and garments–
a shepherd and a hireling
bleat in search of a shepherd.
But the Trojan horse lies in wait.

Words and opposites

I hear them in their yesterday's winding yarns:
We came to efface memories of the past
That which the hawks in powers
Cause us to groan and blame our past choice.
We came that our land will warble her glories
By the brooks and rivulets of our land.
That her citizens be freed
From snarled up anger and hunger of the land.
For every home, each shall be fed
With the milk and honey of the land.

We came to undress looters and their loot
And cast their Garb of looting into a raging furnace.
Our Umbrella pleads for your safety.
In it, neither rain nor sun
Shall cause you scathe.
Our Broom shall sweep away the sorrows of the land.
The South and North shall latch on laughter
And a new dawn of plenitude ...
Ah! Simplicity of rhetoric, service and immolation became
Catch phrases nailed into our ears.
We became wretches of their cherubic
And moral exhortations
In their castle of fibs ...

Rainbows of hope crafted to curry our votes.
Like good shepherds, they came
Like good sheep, we followed.
At last, victory whet their appetite
And a new song echoed.
Hmmm. Pee Dee Pee, Aa Pee Cee

But in today's song:
To their snug, they adjust
And our bones pushed
To the worms of the Earth.
Our dreams impaled, fobbed

Displaced by grassy budget plan
And Serpents turned heroes
cuddling millions.

Like hungry lions, they feast
On our wobbled flesh
Even as our chickens hatch on
the spider's web.

Our faith grew at their promises
But died at their swollen pride,
Their laughters break our heart
And cause our grief swell,
Leaving us with cascades and palliatives of scar.
Hmmn ...
And the poet's words split:
'The politician has two mouths
Both sharp like the white man's razor'.
With words and opposites.

Songs of GADAFI

This rod, the road
This road, the rod
The Libyan road
The Libyan rod.
Ah! the man
The road man
The rod man
Mourn-man GA-DA-FI!

Forty-two gunshots
Forty-two roads
Forty-two rods
Roads of death
Rods of blood
Roads of greed.

Dead wisdom, reasons plagued in options
Option A, I am
Option B, I am
Option C, I am
And voices in Tripoli rising for the ROAD
But the road to freedom, the road to death
Harvesting deaths
And scooping blood
Bloody holidays on carcass of souls
NATO's forces in metallic booms
For the ROAD
Chants of *Allahu Akbar*
Hankering blood in the house of ROD
In the city of Sirte
City of rod
Fallen rod, fallen road.
And the rod rusts
And the road roasts
The red roady, rusty rod
In the tunnel of death

Allahu Akbar!
Allahu Akbar!
Chorus of tears
Bleeding tales
Quires of laughters
Chants of victories
Chants of justice
For breathless souls.

I need a word

I need a word
To swim across the Atlantic Ocean
Erect manses on the Red Sea
Snuggle the sun with a purple kiss
And speak in the moon's tongue.
I need a word.

I need a word
To touch the nipples of Monica
Without Clinton's rod across the sea
Dance *Atilogwu*
In the altar of saints.
I need a word

I need a word
To fly without perching
Move Vatican City, White House and Aso Rock
Atop the heart of Sambisa
Dibble a tittynope of smile
And sing life to a million death.
I need a word.

I need a word
For the ailing land and her weasels,
Healing nations and give Africa a new marque
Her Citizens, the Chosen One,
Her currency, the Special One,
Sought and chased across boundaries.
I need a word
To give wind to my words.

The bawling for Biafra

                    me: An osprey has fouled its own nest.
            to   She
          said   invited
          crane   a
        little   python
        A   to
        And the land wailed.   hoof before its hatchling
        But   And a
          the   red
          phoenix   canary
          asked: sang:
            isn't   that
            that   osprey
              bird   equals
              the   in
              crave   the
              of   wit
                many   and
                down   sapience
                the   of
                hill?   Solomon   king

Death kiss

Visions caged
Missions paused
To chime no more
To weave no more
To dream no more
In the trap of monster kings.

Robed in weapons
Of mass destruction
Detonation their motion
Commotion, their mission
Chaos, their vision.

In the desert of
Raging foes
Raging folks
Raging wars
Trading blood
And scat singing deaths.

But a day beckons
With the sun when
The invisible laughing terror
Today's pang
Shall suspire the breath
Of necrosis
In pieces
Of pains.

Words that muffled the land

They crown us with sainted troth,
in phrases of cornucopia
vowing to tame the colic in us
with seraphic tongues
savaging our hopes
in saintly paroles.

They fill our hearts
with gingerbread;
driving us high
in fertile rain
and soothing sun
but of purging spirits.

Oh brethren!
did you not smell their rats;
the hedgehogs and their
unending games, niggling
throttling tongues and esurient eyes?

Weep not...

Weep not, my son
For the sceptre is aloof to your cries
Blind to your tears
Dumb to your lamentations
Dead to your dreams ...

Weep not, my son
For the sceptre sees no life in your breath
Silent to the tailspin of your dreams
Calm to the hunger gnawing your belly
Benumbed to the bleak sunray

Weep, not my son
For the scepter is deaf to raging agitations
Deaf to the dissonant throbbing of our hearts
Still to your future's pains
Lame to your pain's songs ...

Dashed

my son ...
your cries ...
your tears ...
your lamentations ...
dead to your dreams ...

my son ...
your breath ...
your dreams ...
your belly ...
benumbed to the bleak sunray...

my son ...
raging agitations ...
our hearts ...
future's pains ...
lame to your pain's songs ...

The mongers

Remember …
The limbs
On errands
The blood
That whetted the land
The lives
That groaned beyond
The souls
That went to the Neverland.

Remember …
The hunger
That torments our bellies
The thirst
That exsiccates our tongues
The darkness
That chases our light
The bullets
That chase our breaths
The quakes
That bury our bones
And many lying in the rubble
Remember …

Unwanted songs

I do not want to sing dirges
For the virtues of the land—the fumigations
Of hard work and its bounties at harvests
To many wishes
Of scant effort crowned in abundance
I do not want ...

I do not want to mourn the rogues
Stalking into huts at nightfall
My tears bewailing the loss
Of treasures bequeathed on us,
Tossed and traded by palace dimwits
Whose words and crowns
Drive fears and snivels into our eyes
I do not want ...

I do not want mournful eyes
At the graveside of martyrs
Whose eyes and tongues,
Saw and spoke verity
While grabby tongues
Twisted the tales
For crispy mints
I do not want ...

1 do not want my plaints
truncated in a trice
Hushed to silence
While cowards assail the frontiers
I do not want ...

I do not want melodies of solo beats
And trumpets of *nunc dimitis*
At the demise of truth
While flowering treachery and deceit
Bloom to the glory of plaudits
I do not want ...

I do not want elegy of unrequited love
At holy matrimonies
Sanctified by the congregation and priestly rites
With vacuums wailing for loves
I do not want ...

I do not want the execution of cultures
The perdition of ancestral heritage buried in haste
In exchange of tyrannist modernist songs
To engage the gods in the restorations
Of our royal pride and ancestral blessings.
I do not want ...

I do not want to say blame kismet
For the fate befallen us,
The poverty ravaging us,
In the midst of opulence.
I do not want ... but
The tales of our lands
Broke my vows

Your cast

Before you cast
Sieve their past and sign their days.
Play the old lyrics
Of classical roulades
And cross their thoughts
In present, past and past per principles
In chapters of time.

Before you cast:
Cross their deeds
Of sudden mansions
And their honey pots.
Seek their motions
And unravel their mysteries.

Before you cast
Follow not their tawdry marbles
On caressing lips
And clappers of
Piercing rhetorics on missions
Of burning chase.

Before you cast
Flee from vampires' thirst
Return their smiles and dimple gaze
With suspense and missions
And cast them out
In the booth of destinies.

Parrymentarians

We are the law brea(m)kers
In hallowed chambers
We set the rules
And cage the rules
Official voices
In wagging tongues
If you don't know us
Read us
If you don't read us
See us
Making the laws
And breaking the laws
In deified biffs
Of sacred tongues
We are the laws of the commonwealth
Docked in the house of commotion
Broken bones in building the nations
Role models in comic motions
And raging pollination
Of murky desperation

Soka!

The un/known evil forest
The holocaust of man's heart
With quickened haste
You thump mortal flesh
And sip fellow bloods
In dark corners of mafia lords

Evil careers to the end
In wild chase at noon
The morning breath of terrors
The red deeds at night falls
A syndicate to masters' calls
Blindness coloured the heart
In vein quest
Of tasteless lobes
Of choking comforts
And terror tastes
Of shallow treasures
Darkness seize your souls
In the dungeon of festering hearts
Of poisoned deeds and buried scruples
Held spellbound
To fated men in man's dens
Soka!

Book a ram, kill a ram

Your sacrifice sings for our sorrows
As you truncate our tomorrows
In the wilderness of sleeveless hopes
Singing bifurcations in our homes
Your book is a ram ... book-a-ram?

You plant your druthers
And breed our sorrows
In the dark corners
Of wailing trumpets
Your book is a ram ... book-a-ram?

Your asphyxiation chases a million graves
And stultifies our diversities
You sacrifice your souls
In the vain hopes
Of celestial dividends
Your book is a ram ... book-a-ram?

Listen to the lyrics
Of our orisons
One nation bound in freedom
Peace and unity
And not the strikes
Of your thunderous hurrahs.

The dance

The dice is cast.
The desert's ink has spilled its words
Into the nation's ear
Now, I'm drawn into
An open dance –
The Sahara dance.
Who will dance with me?

It is the dance of
The hunter being hunted
In the forest of death
Splattering its syrups
On my guilty lips.
Who will dance with me?

I am the Dean that knows it all
But didn't know that
Papa named me Dean-no
On the day lyrics
Swept my dance
Into the oxbow of Abu.
Who will dance with me?

My dance sails and sells
Beyond the shores
Into the ivory towers
And city centres –
Harvard, Cambridge, Massachusetts ...
In long stretches
Of certified dance.
Who will dance with me?

Come dance with me
Friends of Ndu and Me.
Come dance with me
Friends of Tin and Ubu.
Come dance with me

Friends of Sir Raki
Or won't you dance with me?

Come dance with me
Friends of Ma and Gu.
Come dance with me
Friends of Bu and Harry.
Or won't you dance with me?

Won't you dance with me
While the dance tickles?
Or you want your face
Smitten on a belly flop
In the rivers
Of Ajekuiya?

Letter to mr president

Dear Baba,
I bring you greetings
From the land of the rising sun
So did the *Agbekoyas*
Transmit tides of compliments.
The pyramids of the North
Spoke well of your benevolence.
Lest I forget,
The oil rigs
Sing your paeans.

Sir, permit me to appraise
That their greetings
Ferret heavy burdens
Of withered smiles
On hungry bellies.
They said:
Your promises of bounty harvests
At the last planting seasons
Lost signs of fruits.
Now, the land mourns
Of failed crops.
Hunger quickens its fangs
On the boulevards of our souls.
Exchanges at market square walk the solitary path
Your warrant chief now imposed gabelle on our lands
Even *aje* has lost her *oriki* on many mouths.

Remember the High Chiefs Adekunle, Ezeamaka and Abass.
Yes, the holy triplets
And their cousins:
Osagie, Dashima and Dashe
Who all cleared the path
To thy rocky palace
Oh! You did?
They said:

Market prices
Now hit the roofs
As our dignified cowries
Cringe at the birth of their dreams.
That:
Farming and drought
Stare us in the face.
The land pleads for the rains
To water the fields
And bless farmers' invocations.
They said:
Many soul brothers
Now test positive
To suicide missions
Than living in Hobbes' nature state.
That cattle herders
Graze our blood and glory
In pursuit of our women and lands.
And many breaths frittered in blood tales,
Of angst and misery, end stops and sorrows …

Today,
Wages
Trickle in bits.
Alas, the palm wine tappers
Wear angry visages along bush tracks.

May the gods
Of our lands
Grace your path
And guide you aright.

We enthuse our love
In motley tongues.
Our regards, too, to
Aunty Kemo and Uncles Babachair, Efele, Kachy
Big brother, Oshy, Nglige and Fash.

Yours faithfully, with heavy eyes,
Akerele Emeka-Salisu.

P.S - Baba do not forget
The next farming seasons
In less
Than twenty-four full moons.

Re: letter to mr president

From the enclave,
Inside the Rock,
Dear Akerele Emeka-Salisu
My ears are filled with muffled sounds
Of our laughters and the stubborn plants
That refuse to grow.

My ears tingle not with
Tales of bountiful harvests but miseries
Of farmers that toil and moil on scablands.
My heart bleeds with lean frames
And famished faces
Amid famines and droughts.

Your voices invaded my equanimity
Shattering knocks, incubus and scabies
Caging my nights and, now, I breathe
Death with scads of anguish.

I am not blind to the thrush
That visits us days and nights
I hear the god of meningitis
Now feasts on our blood. He plants
Desolations on our land
For our sins, so says the chief priest
Of 'Fara' and now death makes
Yurts in our lands …

It is the locusts which swim on our fields
And feast on our greens in times past
That invoke plagues on the bounty harvests
Of our land. We suffer heavy losses
To the rodents in our barns
Who made the palace their oasis.

Hmmmmnn! My heart quakes
At the ruins of our harvests

In time past – a handiwork of hawks
And locusts whose cups
We long to quench our thirsts.

They fiddle our yam tubers and drag bags
Of our cowries to underground tunnels
But let's hail our hunters
Who blew their loot off their hiding crest.
I hear they unearth the caches
In Ikoyi and Sabon Tash
A betokening of stolen harvests.

My laughter and smile have remained quiescent
At the beckon of cascading tears.
Lassitude now cage my bones
My tears now flow like rivers
Searching their source.
My ears blocked with tales of sorrows.
I am now an orphan of queasiness
Chasing healings for the land's woes.

I've been to the white man's land.
And the Queen of the land assembled
Her best medicine men and priestess
Of the land for my bones. Then said she:
'The land's saviour sacrifices himself to it'

I believe not the potency
Of celestial and terrestrial powers
Grinding the bones of palace hosts
So said Abati, the one who split
The Lucky One's words to us in the past.

Tell the Asipas, Umukoros and Danladis
And the labourers of our lands:
Let no one play Judas and sing his death
Across the six villages of our lands.
The bitter leaves shall at last
Succumb to its sweetness

We shall lave our tears
In the rivers of abundance.
Lest I forget,
In the next planting seasons
I shall consult the gods of our lands
And hope my supplications and rituals
For the land's tilling for amplitudes
Replenish my soul and heal my aging ribs

My love for you is dazed with bitter tales.
Accept my smiles under arrest.
My Council of Chiefs – Kachy, Fash
Kemo, Nglige and Big Oshy whose bones
I walk send their greetings.

The table now is
Turned against the chairs.
So Baba chair cannot find his chair
Among my warrant chiefs. I sent him rest
In the village of grass cutters
Where tears chase his smiles ...
Bye

Your servant with painful tales.
Baba.

Letter to mama ... the pains that ache our land

Mother,   Mother,
It is with fright that I weave these lines.   these
My hand dances to the rhythms of grenades   lines
Roaring from enemy turned friends and foes   dance to
Now friends; from armed and armless forces.   the rhythms
                                                        of grenades.

Tell Papa ... that my morning comes
with uneasy tales of bombs shattering and tearing flesh   Morning
like we do to Christmas goats, and blood spuming like Papa's   comes
early morning palm wine. Last night, I saw ghosts   tearing
sipping blood. It reminds me of our cold *kunu* on hot afternoons. flesh
Tell him that I am a snail crawling on dry and fresh   like
Bones cluttered on soils turned ashes and ashes turned soils.   Papa's
Tell my brothers that I have no more tears   ghosts.
To shed. Even death has refused to close my eyes.

I learnt my classmates gained their breath in Dapchi   In Dapchi,
And the nation welcomed their tears.   tears
Now, I alone wander in the forest of death.   wander in
                                                        the forest
Standing before me is life and death;   of death.
Both seeking my flight for their faith.
But I've made love to life, my faith   My faith
And it ferried me to the ocean waves   waves
Lo! The currents smiled, tossed open cheque   open
And asked with a deafening voice saying: cheque
'Will you write your fate or faith   saying:
On this heaven's gate or wait for the petering boat?'   fate
But I replied saying: 'my fate is tied to the Boat of my faith,   or
To the crown and glory, not fate and filth.'   faith?

Mama, something strange happened to me last night.   Last night,
I saw Grandma in my dreams. She walked in silently and sat   walked in
Beside me saying; 'my daughter, life is a bitch   silently
To be sipped in the arms of a beach   and
Not out of reach like many preach'   sat.

Erm … erm … Mother, I'm in a sea of gunshots
swimming in my ears. I hear bawling,
my eyes blurred with garbled flesh

… my life now a tattered book without covers …,
… like a kite lost in the air …
The wind I must obey …
Your daughter,
… Le   h
          a

A sea
        of
          gunshots
              hear
          bawling
              without
                covers.
              The
              air
          I
      must   .
  obey

Trump-Kim ...

The Sun said to the Earth:
With a wink I can clip
Your pennons
Into rings
Of void.

The Earth said to the Sun:
Just my laughter can
Shrink your tongues
Into the hollows
Of silence.

A dance before us

The Earth can clip your pennons
    into
        rings
           of
              Void.

The Sun can shrink your tongues
    into
        the
          hollows
            of
              Silence.

Battle lines ...

My nose smelled the rituals of blood.
My eyes watch angels sail the earth
I saw death and spirits hosted and poised
anthems for old songs
The arguments speak for or against
The cup of glories.
The mighty plead for laughter.
The weak hunt out smiles of many.
Many feet chase a million breaths
Many hands that seek lost ashes

The mask and the masked cravings
Sing the flowerings of the earth.
And we all, worst come off the beat.
In the present, past and futures
Of sane-tenses and sin-tenses
Of words and worlds
Of wars and blood and ...

Red lines

Blood sails the earth
hosted and poised for old songs
   for
       or
          against
Glories for laughter of
  many breaths that
     seek
       lost
         ashes.

the masked cravings of the earth
Come off the beat, past and futures
  and
     sin-
       tenses
         and worlds
          and blood
           and ...

Brothers at war ...   Fissures

Okoro: You, this sly booth you sold me
To the emirate with your tongue speaking both ways
And like chameleon your ways
Blind the eyes and poke the mind.
Out of my way, you this slug
And impervious fellow!

Akin: Blame me not, Okoro, after all
Your brain dances in your mouth
And brags about owning the land with
The black gold. Indeed, you are the
Offspring of the lost tribe wandering
In alien lands with spasmodic attempt
Of a return trait!

Usman: Hold your breath both of you
Have I given you the voice to speak?'
Aren't your destinies a piecemeal
For the sword?'
Now, look at me in the face
And sing, 'The land has come to my feet'

You sold me
   speaking both
                ways.
             Your ways
          poke the mind
    you, this slug fellow.

After all
   your mouth
      land with
         the
            wan-
dering attempt of a return trait.

You speak
   a piecemeal
      for the sword
   in the face, to my feet?

A new song

Yesterday, a new song sprang
Inviting me to a dance
Its melodies so soothing
That my legs cannot
Dance alone.
Yesterday, a type of food emerged
And graced the menu list.
It has taste overshadowing years of
Bitterness.
Yesterday, a new plant emerged
And its flowers sprout with
Certain grandeur so
Riveting for the
Eyes ...
Yesterday, honour traced my path
And chorused, I have come to
Stay with you forever.

Today for tomorrow

I will till the land and make my ridges
I will water the verdures
Today for tomorrow

I will hasten my steps
Unto the doorsteps of sages
Tapping their ups and downs
Growing my trees and not tears
In the height of relevance
Today, for tomorrow!

I will sing the song of time
Make hay with the sun
And scat from pangs of privation
Housed in procrastination
The lazy man's comfort
Not for me, the fainéant tales
Today, for tomorrow.

I will weave my basket now
And carry my future arias
Into the marketplace of hopes
And unbar the nudity
Of soothing grace
Today for tomorrow.

Niger area ...   a country was

I have a country   thrive   A
Where hatred and love thrive.   Love   country
                              And   and
I have a country   country   disunity
Where unity and disunity meld.   A   meld

I have a country   A   A
Where peace and violence melt.   Country   country
                              and   and
I have a country   violence   virtues
Where vices and virtues toast.   melt   toast

I have a country
Where tears and laughter kiss.   OHAFA   for
                              with   better
I have a country   walked   for
Where death and life walked   country   worse
down the aisles with   A   no
Ohaneze, Afenifere and Arewa country   one
Chorusing for better for worse   and   put
And let no one put asunder.   laughter   asunder
                              kiss   a
I have a country,   .   country,
Whose credo is 'There was a Country'   .   there
                                       .   a   was
                                            c
                                             o
                                              u
                                               n
                                                t
                                                 r
                                                  y

Come, laughter come ...   Gone

Come stay with me and make me your nest to roost.
Come stay with me, with the freshness of your taste.
My taste buds certify your flavour worthy of my soul.   Your taste
My soul is a fertile soil for your flowering and harvest.   My soul
Many souls crave your birth and wish the elusiveness of your death.   harvest
Come, come nourish and wax your songs across the earth's face.   Your death
                                        Across the face of the earth
Was man not created for your companion and warmth?
What shall you profit to reject the heart   The heart
That bids you welcome?   Welcome your death
What mouth shall speak the horrors of your death?   That seek
                                        Your warmth
Or to what end is your illusion to many that seek your warmth?

The earth seeks to pay your bride price.
Accept, and oblige the nations' invitation for a toast.   A toast
You cannot claim presbycusis to my pleadings;   my pleadings
Come, come; heal the earth with your winks   your winks
And with your song, make me your sunflowers.   Make me
                                        Your sunflowers.
                                        .

Osun dance of victory

My dance breaks the waist
and boundaries of laughters:
an approval of the body's miles from ataxia
It is a dance of the crown's triumph
and the king's horsemen of Osun.
Indeed, the crown triumphs.

My dance farts, pokes and gladdens
The body and soul of dissidents and adherents of Osun
It feeds many known and unknown eyes
It stinks and births morning and mourning, gain and loss
It is a dance of death and life buried and resurrected.
My death has reincarnated in my dance
Lost and reclaimed on the battlefield of sand, blood and ballot
Indeed, the crown triumphs,

If an injustice rapped my dance and blood
My blood roars for justice and another dance for rebirth
Now justice beams its light and bids injustice goodbye
It is in me to slap after being slapped in the rivals' den
Hope rising … rising and rising
I will dance into a million bills
To plant laughter in my haven
And harvest headlines at my dance
Indeed, the crown triumphs.

To the last end

If haste I must make
If shame I must rake
If love i must hate
If my day must I break
For the hour of glory

Then let my sun
Hasten to rake my shame
And hate my love
At the day's break.

If being, I must unmask
If dreams, I must recall
If truth, I must confess
If light, must I shine
In the dark corners of my naked soul
For the hour of glory

Then let my being say
Recall my dreams
Confess the truth
And shine my light in the dark corners of my naked soul

Nature's smile

As the day births
The birds' wings flung symmetrically
Whirling gracefully, weaving songs of time
And stemming the tide.

The air bids us welcome to the sky
The sky unlocks the moon
The moon surrenders its voice
For our song.

The sun sheds its rays
To the rhythms of the earth's songs.
And freshness echoes our hope
For the songs of many;
And the rhythms of glory made home
Our thoughts with metaphors of hope.

Independence ...   Lost song

<table>
<tr><td>

Your roses sparkled in quizzical notes.
Drum sets across Niger areas, inviting us to a dance
And we all kiss prospects fertile to feed a billion mouths

</td><td>

Quizzical notes
inviting us to a dance
feed a billion mouths.

</td></tr>
<tr><td>

N
Our lands and climates smile with protruding hopes

</td><td>

Smile with protruding
hopes

</td></tr>
<tr><td>

Ready to birth visions and dreams; indeed
Our fields fed the nation's mouths
Our paths decorated with honour across boundaries
And with pride, we proclaim our land and sing her glory
To the envy of many beyond oceans and distant lands.

</td><td>

and dreams indeed
fed the nation's mouths
across boundaries
and sing her glory
beyond oceans ...

</td></tr>
<tr><td>

A
But you arrive too early to the warmth of our prodigals!
I
A cacophony of blindness assaulted our anthems of love,

</td><td>

The warmth of our
prodigals
assaulted our anthems
of   J
love

</td></tr>
<tr><td>

Now, the land is heavy with squandering lords.

</td><td>

With squandering A
lords.

</td></tr>
</table>

How to live ...   illusion

How to live a life without a sin   a life without a sin,
Go to the bank of rivers   bank of rivers
And draw a plat of your shadow.   Of your shadow,
Watch the crabs bat their eyes   bat their eyes
Yank the 't' off the can't   off the can't
And count the spawners' fingerlings in the ocean.   in the ocean

                                                            .
.   .

The pride of laughter

Let my laughter plant
A seed of trade in Aba;
That many that buy shall make dinner
And grace the night with happy rest craving the day's birth.

Not the laughter mixed with salt and sugar
And euphemisms, decorating the naked lines of Sambisa.
Let my laughter paint
The colours of freedom like October First
And let me plant and harvest the land's abundance.
Not the emperors' laughter of dust and smoke;
Trading souls offshore and counting gains of life and death.

Let my laughter smell
the aroma of Joshua's jabs
Kissing Klitscko at the eleventh round.
Not laughters proclaiming
Victory over 'infidels' on 9/11…

Let my laughter dance
To lovers of craft with memories

Of Kongi's harvest of songs made hands
Rhyme and gave Africa a new name in Stockholm city;
Not laughters baked with blood
Against insurgents of Biafra, Somalia, Rwanda, Libya, Syria, Iraq…

Let my laughter adorn the royal beads
Across the globe like Messi's refrain
And Ronaldo's lyrics of Ballon'd'Or
Not volcanic eruptions of laughters
Welcoming the brides of Chibok to my thighs
Nor bleedings and atomic tales of blood in Burma,
Sambisa, Hiroshima … all clinging to the dust of the earth.

Plant Aba
make dinner
with happy rest
Craving the day's
birth
with salt and sugar.
Lines of Sambisa
paint October first
and harvest the land's abundance
of dust and smoke
counting the gains of life and
death
Smell Joshua's
jabs
At the eleventh round
proclaiming infidels

On 9/11

Dance with memories
Of songs made hands
in Stockholm
baked with blood
Against Biafran insurgents…
Adorn the royal beads
like messi's refrain.
Lyrics of Ballon'd'or

Laughters of Chibok
to my thighs
in Burma
Sambisa
to the
dust
of the
earth

Lost

Bring back our days when virginity
the pride of wedding nights. And
virginity mortals feed many mouths
with metaphors of pride. And merry strikes
our ludi saeculares with bridal songs
to in-laws' glory and pride.

Bring back our days when birds
unguided make nests. Our light
clips the lips of darkness and truth
overcoming shadows.
Our men stand firm on words and honours;
women keep their homes.
And children, the innocent hopes of our lands,
and the land dances with us.

Bring back our days
When leaders are heroes, and followers, sages
And both cling to struggle and persevere with
Blood and thirst for the land's
songs, victories and honours.

Today
Street hawks feast on the nakedness of our brides
Darkness now guest of honour; the future breeds tears
Shepherds rake the land of its sweetness and tag us fusspots
The sheep chorus songs of bitterness with killer instincts
And now the land cracks our hopes leavings us with its fissures.

2019

Before reincarnating the pratfalls of old
Let the mahatmas and custodians,

Of our land and history
Sing our past and past tense.
Shall we sing the doom of the past
And cross yet another path of thunder

Which danced affright on us all?
Yet, the swivet poses for another rebirth.

2023?

Will they stitch the flesh
mangled by tyrants of yesteryear?
Will they fill the holes of our hearts
And mend our broken bones rammed into ashes?
Will our light coruscate again and visions restored?
Or shall again, we, nailed to the fictions
Of fairy tales …?

2015?

the pratfalls of old, mahatmas and
custodians
of past and past tense, sing the doom
of the past.
Another
path of thunder danced affright on
us all.
The swivet poses for another
rebirth.

2019

The flesh of yesteryear,
our hearts, rammed into ashes.
And visions restored to the
fictions of
fairy
tales …

Petepete ...   the pain of our hearts

May their bones dance to the frenzy
Of a raging forest;   the frenzy forest
They, who promised us smile but water   water the
The pain of our hearts.   pain
                                 of

May their flesh haste to the python's belly;   our
They who muffle our breath with farts of odium   hearts.
Riding horses without history.   The python's belly
                         Breathe with

May their hours of honour fling open   arts
Their doors of shame;   of odium without history.
They who sign our deaths at closed doors
And dine with us at lunch time.   Honour flung open shame
                      At closed doors and dine

May they welcome the land's curse;   with us at
They, who raise our hopes in public glare but puddle   lunch
Our sorrows and tales at dusk.   Time.
                The land's curse puddle
                         tales
                           at
                             dusk.

Hard lines ...   Red lines

The rain has refused to wipe away
The tears of the sun.
The moon chooses its own light
In the glare of the sun's rays
And said: I have my tales to tell
When the sun's tears are dry.

                    wipe away the sun
                        its own light
                            the sun's rays
                                tell
                                    when
                                        the sun's tears
                                            are
                                                d
                                                    r
                                                        y
                                                            .
                                                                .
                                                                    .

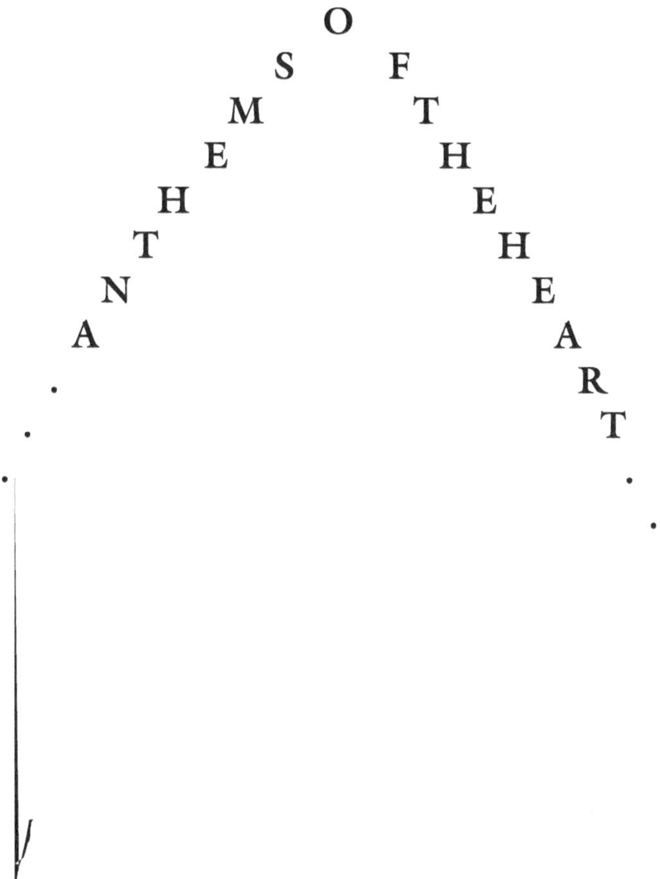
ANTHEMS OF THE HEART

Heart beats

     Ifunanya,
the   is
door   ajar
of   for
my   your
heart   warmth

Enter ...
   enter
        not as
          a guest
            but ...

But
like a trogon
 re
       tur
         ning
           to

its
nest.

Silent night

Though your love puts me behind the bar,
I remember the day
Your saliva met mine
Draining my thoughts
Into your breath.

It sweetened my soul
In fragrance of melting heart
Of quivering beat
And humming breath.

My motion
Drives me to your gaze
And slowly we
Unmask our being
In silent night
Of voiceless voice
And tasteful tales …

Ify

You invited me to the hues
Of your heart
Make me your songs
That my tongue shall wax
Lullabies of the heart
And make you the rivers
Of my love.

Do not say no to my lyrics
That mellow the heart
That my mitts shall stick to your ribs
Breaking boundaries of your waist
In za oza rum

I am a freeborn of love
And you my apple

All I crave is:
Lead me to the door
Of your heart
That I may plant and water the
Seed of your love
In cupid's garden.

That the fragrance
Of your love digs a well
In my heart
Is an understatement

If only you can
Make me the anthem
Of your heart
That my soul shall sing.

Emeka's chase

I told my mama
That I want to marry Ada
And she said:
If her thighs are not wide open
Bring her home ...

But papa said:
My son, even if her pot
Is deep but
Quickens the fermentation
Of your wine
And she can tweak
Her heart with
Golden thoughts
Plant a kiss on her
It is with my blessings.

Mascara

Upon this face I rest the frailties of lulu;
Take not my part for with me, the lady's touch on point.

Feed me the essential supplements for the eyes to behold,
Praying new catches come by. But it seems their eyes are
Blind to a million calls and their tongues gabbled and vapid.
Come, part me not, follow not –
their stubborn tongues against our splurge.

Welcome! Night sues your divorce.
And now, you must part on my soap bubbles.
Don't worry. This night kills our dream
But trust, tomorrow births your day for a tale.

Sayonara

I have planted my words into   Into
the earth's soul   the earth's
And the tales it spuds   soul,
Farewell to all tyrant and faithful,   spuds
Loyalists of the word and the world it rebirths.   faithful
                                                 rebirths.

Kraftgriots

Also in the series (POETRY) *continued*

g'ebinyŏ ogbowei: *let the honey run & other poems* (2005)
Joe Ushie: *Popular Stand & Other Poems* (2005)
Gbemisola Adeoti: *Naked Soles* (2005)
Aj. Dagga Tolar: *This Country is not a Poem* (2005)
Tunde Adeniran: *Labyrinthine Ways* (2006)
Sophia Obi: *Tears in a Basket* (2006)
Tonyo Biriabebe: *Undercurrents* (2006)
Ademola O. Dasylva: *Songs of Odamolugbe* (2006), winner, 2006 ANA/Cadbury poetry prize
George Ehusani: *Flames of Truth* (2006)
Abubakar Gimba: *This Land of Ours* (2006)
g'ebinyŏ ogbowei: *the heedless ballot box* (2006)
Hyginus Ekwuazi: *Love Apart* (2006), winner, 2007 ANA/NDDC Gabriel Okara poetry prize
    and winner, 2007 ANA/Cadbury poetry prize
Abubakar Gimba: *Inner Rumblings* (2006)
Albert Otto: *Letters from the Earth* (2007)
Aj. Dagga Tolar: *Darkwaters Drunkard* (2007)
Idris Okpanachi: *The Eaters of the Living* (2007), winner, 2008 ANA/Cadbury poetry prize
Tubal-Cain: *Mystery in Our Stream* (2007), winner, 2006 ANA/NDDC Gabriel Okara poetry
    prize
John Iwuh: *Ashes & Daydreams* (2007)
Sola Owonibi: *Chants to the Ancestors* (2007)
Adewale Aderinale: *The Authentic* (2007)
Ebi Yeibo: *The Forbidden Tongue* (2007)
Doutimi Kpakiama: *Salute to our Mangrove Giants* (2008)
Halima M. Usman: *Spellbound* (2008)
Hyginus Ekwuazi: *Dawn Into Moonlight: All Around Me Dawning* (2008), winner, 2008 ANA/
    NDDC Gabriel Okara poetry prize
Ismail Bala Garba & Abdullahi Ismaila (eds.): *Pyramids: An Anthology of Poems from North-
    ern Nigeria* (2008)
Denja Abdullahi: *Abuja Nunyi (This is Abuja)* (2008)
Japhet Adeneye: *Poems for Teenagers* (2008)
Seyi Hodonu: *A Tale of Two in Time (Letters to Susan)* (2008)
Ibukun Babarinde: *Running Splash of Rust and Gold* (2008)
Chris Ngozi Nkoro: *Trails of a Distance* (2008)
Tunde Adeniran: *Beyond Finalities* (2008)
Abba Abdulkareem: *A Bard's Balderdash* (2008)
Ifeanyi D. Ogbonnaya: *... And Pigs Shall Become House Cleaners* (2008)
g'ebinyŏ ogbowei: *the town crier's song* (2009)
g'ebinyŏ ogbowei: *song of a dying river* (2009)
Sophia Obi-Apoko: *Floating Snags* (2009)
Akachi Adimora-Ezeigbo: *Heart Songs* (2009), winner, 2009 ANA/Cadbury poetry prize
Hyginus Ekwuazi: *The Monkey's Eyes* (2009)
Seyi Adigun: *Prayer for the Mwalimu* (2009)
Faith A. Brown: *Endless Season* (2009)
B.M. Dzukogi: *Midnight Lamp* (2009)
B.M. Dzukogi: *These Last Tears* (2009)
Chimezie Ezechukwu: *The Nightingale* (2009)
Ummi Kaltume Abdullahi: *Tiny Fingers* (2009)

Ismaila Bala & Ahmed Maiwada (eds.): *Fireflies: An Anthology of New Nigerian Poetry* (2009)

Eugenia Abu: *Don't Look at Me Like That* (2009)

Data Osa Don-Pedro: *You Are Gold and Other Poems* (2009)

Sam Omatseye: *Mandela's Bones and Other Poems* (2009)

Sam Omatseye: *Dear Baby Ramatu* (2009)

C.O. Iyimoga: *Fragments in the Air* (2010)

Bose Ayeni-Tsevende: *Streams* (2010)

Seyi Hodonu: *Songs from My Mother's Heart (2010),* winner ANA/NDDC Gabriel Okara poetry prize, 2010

Akachi Adimora-Ezeigbo: *Waiting for Dawn* (2010)

Hyginus Ekwuazi: *That Other Country* (2010), winner, ANA/Cadbury poetry prize, 2010

Emmanuel Frank-Opigo: *Masks and Facades* (2010)

Tosin Otitoju: *Comrade* (2010)

Arnold Udoka: *Poems Across Borders* (2010)

Arnold Udoka: *The Gods Are So Silent & Other Poems* (2010)

Abubakar Othman: *The Passions of Cupid* (2010)

Okinba Launko: *Dream-Seeker on Divining Chain* (2010)

'kufre ekanem: *the ant eaters* (2010)

McNezer Fasehun: *Ever Had a Dear Sister* (2010)

Baba S. Umar: *A Portrait of My People* (2010)

Gimba Kakanda: *Safari Pants* (2010)

Sam Omatseye: *Lion Wind & Other Poems* (2011)

Ify Omalicha: *Now that Dreams are Born* (2011)

Karo Okokoh: *Souls of a Troubadour* (2011)

Ada Onyebuenyi, Chris Ngozi Nkoro, Ebere Chukwu (eds): *Uto Nka: An Anthology of Literature for Fresh Voices* (2011)

Mabel Osakwe: *Desert Songs of Bloom* (2011)

Pious Okoro: *Vultures of Fortune & Other Poems* (2011)

Godwin Yina: *Clouds of Sorrows* (2011)

Nnimmo Bassey: *I Will Not Dance to Your Beat* (2011)

Denja Abdullahi: *A Thousand Years of Thirst* (2011)

Enoch Ojotisa: *Commoner's Speech* (2011)

Rowland Timi Kpakiama: *Bees and Beetles* (2011)

Lawrence Ogbo Ugwuanyi: *Let Them Not Run* (2011)

Saddiq M. Dzukogi: *Canvas* (2011)

Arnold Udoka: *Running with My Rivers* (2011)

Olusanya Bamidele: *Erased Without a Trace* (2011)

Olufolake Jegede: *Treasure Pods* (2012)

Karo Okokoh: *Songs of a Griot* (2012), winner. ANA/NDDC Gabriel Okara poetry prize, 2012

Musa Idris Okpanachi: *From the Margins of Paradise* (2012)

John Martins Agba: *The Fiend and Other Poems* (2012)

Sunnie Ododo: *Broken Pitchers* (2012)

'Kunmi Adeoti: *Epileptic City* (2012)

Ibiwari Ikiriko: *Oily Tears of the Delta* (2012)

Bala Dalhatu: *Moonlights* (2012)

Karo Okokoh: *Manna for the Mind* (2012)

Chika O. Agbo: *The Fury of the Gods* (2012)

Emmanuel C. S. Ojukwu: *Beneath the Sagging Roof* (2012)

Amirikpa Oyigbenu: *Cascades and Flakes* (2012)

Ebi Yeibo: *Shadows of the Setting Sun* (2012)

Chikaoha Agoha: *Shreds of Thunder* (2012)

Mark Okorie: *Terror Verses* (2012)
Clemmy Igwebike-Ossi: *Daisies in the Desert* (2012)
Idris Amali: *Back Again (At the Foothills of Greed)* (2012)
A.N. Akwanya: *Visitant on Tiptoe* (2012)
Akachi Adimora-Ezeigbo: *Dancing Masks* (2013)
Chinazo-Bertrand Okeomah: *Furnace of Passion* (2013)
g'ebinyŏ ogbowei: *marsh boy and other poems* (2013)
Ifeoma Chinwuba: *African Romance* (2013)
Remi Raji: *Sea of my Mind* (2013)
Francis Odinya: *Never Cry Again in Babylon* (2013)
Immanuel Unekwuojo Ogu: *Musings of a Pilgrim* (2013)
Khabyr Fasasi: *Tongues of Warning* (2013)
J.C.P. Christopher: *Salient Whispers* (2014)
Paul T. Liam: *Saint Sha'ade and other poems* (2014)
Joy Nwiyi: *Burning Bottom* (2014)
R. Adebayo Lawal: *Melodreams* (2014)
R. Adebayo Lawal: *Music of the Muezzin* (2014)
Idris Amali: *Efeega: War of Ants* (2014)
Samuel Onungwe: *Tantrums of a King* (2014)
Bizuum G. Yadok: *Echoes of the Plateau* (2014)
Abubakar Othman: *Bloodstreams in the Desert* (2014)
rome aboh: *a torrent of terror* (2014)
Udenta O. Udenta: *37 Seasons Before the Tornado* (2015)
Magnus Abraham-Dukuma: *Dreams from the Creek* (2015)
Christian Otobotekere: *The Sailor's Son 1* (2015)
Tanure Ojaide: *Tale of the Harmattan* (2015)
Festus Okwekwe: *Our Mother is Not a Woman* (2015)
Tunde Adeniran: *Fate and Faith* (2015)
Khabyr Fasasi: *Spells of Solemn Songs* (2015)
Chris Anyokwu: *Naked Truth* (2015)
Zoya Jibodu: *Melodies of Love* (2015)
Tanure Ojaide: *Songs of Myself: Quartet* (2015)
Rita Nsiegbe: *Pool of Love* (2016)
Ade Ajakaiye: *Fire in my Soul* (2016)
Toyin Shittu: *Naija Blues and Other Poems* (2016)
Abdul-Rasheed Na'Allah: *Obama Mentum* (2016)
Obi Nwakanma: *Birthcry* (2016)
Okejoto Gochua: *Choruses from the Waterfront* (2016)
Camarade: *I am a Storyteller* (2016)
Aanuoluwapo John Adesina: *Emocean* (2016)
Amina Aboje: *Promises on Sand* (2016)
Charles Akinsete: *Do Not Preach to Me!* (2017)
Olumide Olaniyan: *Lucidity of Absurdity* (2017)
Ikeogu Oke: *The Heresiad* (2017)
El-Mubashir Abdulsalam: *Hope Still for My Raped Land* (2017)
Psalms Chinaka: *Apocalyptic Gong* (2017)
Seyi Adigun: *A Child of Smell* (2017)
Ebi Yeibo: *Of Waters and The Wild* (2017)
Harry Garuba: *Animist Chants and Memorials* (2017)
Femi Adedina: *The Communique* (2017)
Kola Eke: *October 1960 and Other Poems* (2018)
Tanure Ojaide: *The Questioner: New Poems* (2018)
Aj. Dagga Tolar: *Dissick Republic* (2018)

Joe Ushie: *Tsunami Blues & Other Poems* (2018)
Joe Ushie: *Yawns and Belches* (2018)
Ugoka Chiamaka Amalachukwu: *I Don't Need Your Pity: Collection of Sounds and Motions* (2018)
Ernest Nnamdi Onuoha: *Beauty in the Rubble* (2018)
Sunday Okpanachi: *So Long a Journey* (2019)